Wiccan Chants

By Christine Roche

PDP Publications
www.PDPPublications.info

Copyright 2012 - Christine Roche. All Rights Reserved. No Part of this book may be reproduced in any manner whatsoever, including Internet usage, without the written permission from PDP Publications except in the case of brief quotations embodied in articles and reviews.

First Edition

First Printing 2012

Cover Art by J. Witt

Contents

Introduction 5
To Focus Chant 6
Summoning Spirits Chant 6
Freedom Chant 7
Protection from Evil Chant 7
Daily Protection Chant 7
Release your Own Negativity Chant 8
Banish Negativity from Someone Else Chant 8
Banish an Entity 9
Invoke Energy 9
Healing Chant 9
Remove Stress from Oneself Chant 10
To Gain Courage Chant 10
Calming Chant 11
Get Money Chant 11
Healing Yourself Chant 12
Weight loss Chant 12
Gain Insight Chant 12
Self- Image Chant 13
Recover a Lost Item Chant 13
Friendship Chant 13
Harvest Time Chant 14
Prevent a Nightmare Chant 14
Go to Sleep Chant 14
Bring Happiness to Yourself Chant 15
Breakup Chant 15
To Bring Bodily Warmth Chant 16
To Bring Bodily Coolness Chant 16
Rid Yourself of a Fever Chant 16
Rid Yourself of a Headache Chant 17

Honest Communication with a Partner Chant	17
Pregnancy Chant	18
Child Protection Chant	18
The Witches' Chant by Lady Sheba	19
Goddess Chant	20
God Chant	20
The Wiccan Rede (Short Version)	21
The Wiccan Rede (Long Version)	22

Introduction

The sacred art of chanting is a practice as old as time itself, involving the use of words and phrases in an attempt to bolster ones spiritual development.

Many ancient and modern religions use chants as part of their own religious culture.

In Wicca, chanting is used to raise the energy within oneself to achieve a goal or task. It allows one to align with the god or goddesses consciousness then imbuing that consciousness into their own being. Chanting sends energy to the spiritual realm in order to manifest change in the physical realm. Chanting will also assist with focusing your mind on whatever it is you are looking to achieve.

When chanting, it is very important to have complete faith in the recitation of the chant being used. It is primarily through faith - aided by a strong will - that you achieve your goals.

The chants provided in this book are powerful, yet simple to memorize and simple to use. These chants can be used as is, or they can be incorporated into a spell or ritual.

To Focus Chant
Quiet My Mind

Please be Still

Focus on What All that I Will

No Scattering or Dissension

I Order You, Please Pay Attention

Bring Clear Focus, To My Mind

Grant Me Clarity until my Work is Complete

Summoning Spirits Chant
Spirits Hear Me Sit and Cry

I Summon You from the Other Side

Come to Me

Cross the great divide

Freedom Chant

Wherever I Go

Wherever I Be

Always Know

My Life is Free

Protection from Evil Chant

Divine Goddess, Divine God

If Evil dwells within this place

Please make it leave my space

Daily Protection Chant

I am Protected by the Might

Gracious Goddess

Day and Night

Hold me Safe

From the Harm

Make me feel nice and warm

Release your Own Negativity Chant
From the Earth

Into the Sky

Release my Negativity

Allow it to Fly

Banish Negativity from Someone Else Chant
To the God and Goddess, I do pray

Grant me power, strength to stay

Remove their Curse

Make it begone

With these words

I hold thee at bay

Banish an Entity

My body is not yours to approach

My steps are not yours to follow

In my home, you shall stay away

In my shadows you will not play

I banish you from my life

Stay away, feel my might

Invoke Energy

EKO, EKO, AZARAK, EKO, EKO, ZOMELAK,

EKO, EKO, CERNUNNOS, EKO, EKO, ARADIA

Healing Chant

This chant I hereby Intone,

Heal these wounds

Bone to Bone

End to End

Wounds become whole again

Remove Stress from Oneself Chant

Storms within

Storms without

Storms above

Storms below

In my center

Stillness lies

It is my will

It is my right

To Gain Courage Chant

The meek are weak

Give me strength

Courage above All

The meek are weak

Calming Chant
I am peaceful, I am strong

When day follows night,

Peace in my life

Will be alright

I am always safe from harm,

Goddess hold me in your arms

Get Money Chant
Green glows

Money flows

Into my pockets

Into my purse

Green glows

Money flows

Healing Yourself Chant

The healing touch of Goddess light,

My health grows strong

Fill me with your might

Weight loss Chant

Goddess, Goddess

Make me thin

Shine your beauty into my skin

When I sleep

I will become a thin

Gain Insight Chant

Divine Mother

Mother Divine

Show me the Way

Give me a sign

Self- Image Chant
Blessed Goddess

Flame so bright

Bring me change

Every night

Give me now my second chance

My beauty and glamour

Please enhance

Recover a Lost Item Chant
I now invoke the law of three

What once was lost

Come back to me

Friendship Chant
God and Goddess hear our plea,

Make our friendship stronger be,

Unified together, my friend and me

Harvest Time Chant
Boughs they Shake and Bells Do Ring

Merrily Comes Our Harvest In

Ploughed and Sowed

We've Reaped, We've Mowed

Merrily, Merrily Our Harvest Is In

Prevent a Nightmare Chant
Evil dreams go away

Never are you what you seem

Go away

Far, far away

Leave my dreams

Do not stay

Go to Sleep Chant
Into the dark of night

Allow my mind to drift in flight

Dream, dreams of things to come

Until I wake with to the rising sun

Bring Happiness to Yourself Chant

Happiness and glee

Take my anger, it must flee

Forever and ever more

Make my happiness ever so clear

Everlasting, joyful tears

When this chant comes to past

Make my happiness come to me fast

Breakup Chant

Love once held our bonds

I now choose

To tread a different path

To cast away the union we had

Bittersweet though our parting may be,

Allow my heart and soul be free.

To Bring Bodily Warmth Chant

I am warm,

Warm as fire,

All this warmth is my desire.

To Bring Bodily Coolness Chant

I am cold,

Cold as ice,

All this freezing is my desire

Rid Yourself of a Fever Chant

Fever go away from me

I give it, water, unto thee

Unto me thou art not dear

Therefore go away from here

To where they nursed thee

Where they shelter thee,

Where they love thee

Mashurdalo—help!

Rid Yourself of a Headache Chant

Oh, pain in my head

The father of all evil

Look upon me now!

Thou hast greatly pained me

Thou torments my head

Remain not in me!

Go thou, go thou, go home

Whence thou, Evil One

Thither, thither hasten!

Who treads upon my shadow

To him give this pain!

Honest Communication with a Partner Chant

Air we breathe

Flowing through me

Let us speak with honesty

Pregnancy Chant

To you my child, my body is open,

To you my child, my mind is open.

To you my child, my heart is open.

By Earth, Fire, Wind, and Sea,

Into my arms you will be.

Child Protection Chant

Protect my child

On this Day

Watch over him/her as he/she plays

Make this day safe all the way

Watch my child all throughout the day

The Witches' Chant by Lady Sheba

Darksome night and shining moon,

Hearken to the witches' rune.

East then South, West then North,

Hear! Come! I call thee forth!

By all the powers of land and sea,

Be obedient unto me.

Wand and Pentacle and Sword,

Hearken ye unto my word.

Cords and Censer, Scourge and Knife,

Waken all ye into life.

Powers of the witch's Blade,

Come ye as the charge is made.

Queen of Heaven, Queen of Hell,

Send your aid unto the spell.

Horned Hunter of the night,

Work my will by magic rite.

By all the powers of land and sea,

As I do say, "So mote it be."

By all the might of moon and sun,

As I do will, it shall be done.

Goddess Chant

Isis, Astarte, Diana, Hecate

Demeter, Kali, Inanna

God Chant

Pan, Herne, Osiris, Priapus

Ba'al, Dioysis, Apolo, Lugh

The Wiccan Rede (Short Version)

Bide the Wiccan Laws ye must

In perfect love and perfect trust.

Eight words the Wiccan Rede fufill,

An ye harm none, do what ye will.

Lest in thy self-defense it be,

Ever mind the rule of three.

Follow this in mind and heart,

And Merry Meet and Merry Part!

The Wiccan Rede (Long Version)

Bide within the Law you must, in perfect Love and perfect Trust.
Live you must and let to live, fairly take and fairly give.

For tread the Circle thrice about to keep unwelcome spirits out.
To bind the spell well every time, let the spell be said in rhyme.

Light of eye and soft of touch, speak you little, listen much.
Honor the Old Ones in deed and name,
let love and light be our guides again.

Deosil go by the waxing moon, chanting out the joyful tune.
Widdershins go when the moon doth wane,
and the werewolf howls by the dread wolfsbane.

When the Lady's moon is new, kiss the hand to Her times two.
When the moon rides at Her peak then your heart's desire seek.

Heed the North winds mighty gale, lock the door and trim the sail.
When the Wind blows from the East, expect the new and set the feast.

When the wind comes from the South, love will kiss you on the mouth.
When the wind whispers from the West, all hearts will find peace and rest.

Nine woods in the Cauldron go, burn them fast and burn them slow.
Birch in the fire goes to represent what the Lady knows.

Oak in the forest towers with might, in the fire it brings the God's insight. Rowan is a tree of power causing life and magick to flower.

Willows at the waterside stand ready to help us to the Summerland.

Hawthorn is burned to purify and to draw faerie to your eye.

Hazel-the tree of wisdom and learning adds its strength to the bright fire burning.
White are the flowers of Apple tree that brings us fruits of fertility.

Grapes grow upon the vine giving us both joy and wine.
Fir does mark the evergreen to represent immortality seen.

Elder is the Lady's tree burn it not or cursed you'll be.
Four times the Major Sabbats mark in the light and in the dark.

As the old year starts to wane the new begins, it's now Samhain.
When the time for Imbolc shows watch for flowers through the snows.

When the wheel begins to turn soon the Beltane fires will burn.
As the wheel turns to Lamas night power is brought to magick rite.

Four times the Minor Sabbats fall use the Sun to mark them all.
When the wheel has turned to Yule light the log the Horned One rules.

In the spring, when night equals day time for Ostara to come our way.
When the Sun has reached its height time for Oak and Holly to fight.

Harvesting comes to one and all when the Autumn Equinox does fall.
Heed the flower, bush, and tree by the Lady blessed you'll be.

Where the rippling waters go cast a stone, the truth you'll know.
When you have and hold a need, harken not to others greed.

With a fool no season spend or be counted as his friend.
Merry Meet and Merry Part bright the cheeks and warm the heart.

Mind the Three-fold Laws you should three times bad and three times good.
When misfortune is now wear the star upon your brow.

Be true in love this you must do unless your love is false to you.

These Eight words the Rede fulfill:

"An Ye Harm None, Do What Ye Will"

_____

Thank You

Thank you for purchasing this book from PDP Publications. As a special thank you we'd like to provide you with this coupon for $5 off any $20 purchase at

http://www.ritualmagick.net

Use Coupon Code:

REF451

PDP Publications
www.PDPPublications.info

Copyright 2012 - Christine Roche. All Rights Reserved. No Part of this book may be reproduced in any manner whatsoever, including Internet usage, without the written permission from PDP Publications except in the case of brief quotations embodied in articles and reviews.

First Edition

First Printing 2012

Cover Art by J. Witt

More Wiccan Books from PDP Publications

The Witches Book of Spells

The Modern Day Spellbook

The Wiccan Guide to Candle Magic

Witches in the Kitchen: Recipes for the Eight Sabbats

ARADIA, or the Gospel of the Witches

CPSIA information can be obtained
at www.ICGtesting.com
Printed in the USA
LVOW02s1741020317
525958LV00014B/333/P

9 781475 190007